Start showing up to your Bliss Life.

The 6 Relationships that make up your Bliss Life are:

Self
Higher Power
Tribe
Network
Money
Time

Your Bliss Life will forever be in constant flow, and sometimes one Relationship will take precedence over another. Just like Maslow's Hierarchy of Needs, you'll need to set a foundation in your relationships before transcending to the next level.

Your foundation is Self. Self-awareness is the key to unlocking a Bliss Life. Having a strong sense of Self and being able to attune to the needs of Self will set the stage for all your wildest dreams to come true.

If you don't know yourself, your wants, needs, fears, and desires, you'll never know what you truly want. And if you don't know what you want, how can you live a life that fills you with Bliss?

The greatest way to start building a relationship with yourself is to journal. Journaling is one of the most powerful tools we have in creating a Bliss Life.

You can start very simply. Write a list of 100 things you like. This is the Wild West of journaling; there are no rules here. Nothing is off-limits. No one has to read this list except you, so don't feel required to list things you think you *should*, but do be specific.

1. _____

2. _____

3. _____

4. _____

5. _____

6. _____

7. _____

8. _____

9. _____

10. _____

11. _____

12. _____

13. _____

14. _____

15. _____

16. _____

17. _____

18. _____

19. _____

20. _____

21. _____

22. _____

23. _____

24. _____

25. _____

26. _____

27. _____

28. _____

29. _____

30. _____

31. _____
32. _____
33. _____
34. _____
35. _____
36. _____
37. _____
38. _____
39. _____
40. _____
41. _____
42. _____
43. _____
44. _____
45. _____
46. _____
47. _____
48. _____

49. _____
50. _____
51. _____
52. _____
53. _____
54. _____
55. _____
56. _____
57. _____
58. _____
59. _____
60. _____
61. _____
62. _____
63. _____
64. _____
65. _____
66. _____

67. _____
68. _____
69. _____
70. _____
71. _____
72. _____
73. _____
74. _____
75. _____
76. _____
77. _____
78. _____
79. _____
80. _____
81. _____
82. _____
83. _____

84. _____
85. _____
86. _____
87. _____
88. _____
89. _____
90. _____
91. _____
92. _____
93. _____
94. _____
95. _____
96. _____
97. _____
98. _____
99. _____
100. _____

This list will give you tremendous insight into your relationship with your Self.

Practice self-awareness and take notice of yourself. Do most of your favorite things include being social or anti-social?

Your Bliss Life will then have you prioritizing time for more (or less) social activities. Seeing a lot of outdoor adventures on your lists? Time with animals? A need to work towards a higher social purpose, higher paychecks, or both?

Once you have gotten into a habit of daily journaling, take it to the next level with journal prompts. There are millions of lists and blog articles, books, and other resources you can use to find some self-discovery prompts.

Here are a few to get you started…

What are some ways I've achieved success?

_____
_____
_____
_____
_____
_____

What gets me excited?

_____
_____
_____
_____
_____
_____

What would be my perfect day?

_____
_____

_____
_____
_____
_____

When do I feel the most proud of myself?

_____
_____
_____
_____
_____

When do I usually give up?

_____
_____
_____
_____
_____

What did my life look like when I was the happiest? How is it now?

_____
_____

_____

_____

_____

_____

What activities drain me?

_____

_____

_____

_____

_____

How can I stretch my comfort zone?

_____

_____

_____

_____

_____

You are looking to build a relationship with Self, so treat yourself like someone you really want to have a relationship with. Get to know your likes and dislikes and spend time treating Self with love, grace, and a little extra attention when you need it.

Get to know who you are and what you truly want. This is the longest and most committed relationship you will ever have, fostering the relationship with Self continuously. This is the first step to creating Bliss Life. Envisioning a Bliss Life, a life you're happy to wake up to every day, gives you a target to aim at, a direction to follow.

Knowing specifically what you want provides clarity in decision-making.

Remember your self-awareness and begin to see your goal in the distance.

The fastest way to identify your first steps towards your Bliss Life goal and get better acquainted with how you want to feel is to think back to a time when you felt the most successful.

Use these prompts to get clear about the time in your life you felt the most successful.

When in my life have I felt the most successful?

_____
_____
_____
_____
_____
_____

What did my life look like then?

_____
_____

_____
_____
_____
_____

How was I spending my time? How did I feel?

_____
_____
_____
_____
_____

Where was I working and living? How did I feel about my situation then?

_____
_____
_____
_____
_____

Who was I spending time with? How did those relationships make me feel?

_____
_____

_____

_____

_____

_____

How was I making and spending money? How did that make me feel?

_____

_____

_____

_____

_____

What was I doing with my free time? How did those activities make me feel?

_____

_____

_____

_____

_____

How close was I then to my version of a Bliss Life?

_____

_____

_____
_____
_____
_____

Compare that time of your life to now.

What has shifted in my current state of being and feeling?

_____
_____
_____
_____
_____
_____

What elements of that time would I like to bring back?

_____
_____
_____
_____
_____

What can I do right now to regain that feeling of success?

_____
_____
_____
_____
_____

When it comes to setting your goals, you must make up your mind with absolute certainty, "This is what I want." Do you really want to have a Bliss Life? Then commit to doing whatever it takes.

DECIDE how you want to feel. DECIDE to change your life, your circumstances, your waistline, or the number in your bank account. If you're not committed to the change, why "try"? Why go through the motions half-heartedly?

And so, to begin this process for yourself, start with the most important questions. Answer them truthfully. Remember, this is YOUR Bliss Life, not your mother, partner, or someone on Instagram telling you what your life should be like. But you, getting courageously honest about what you want.

How do I want to feel?

Who do I want to be?

The answers to these questions should be broad and general.

EXAMPLES:
I want to **feel** healthy.
I want to **be** someone who is in great shape.

I want to **feel** calm and intentional.
I want to **be** someone who has a consistent morning and evening routine and who's always ready for the day ahead.

I want to **feel** financially secure.
I want to **be** someone who manages their money well.

The next step in figuring out your goals is to identify what that person (who will soon be you) actually does. This is where you get incredibly specific about your goals.

Take your goals through this checklist as each element will build upon the next. Use the next few pages to brainstorm several goals for yourself.

1. Emotional — How do I want to feel?

_____
_____
_____
_____

2. Personal — Who do I want to be? How do I define the feeling of who I want to be?

_____
_____
_____
_____

3. Literal — What I am specifically going to do to feel and be that person?

_____
_____
_____
_____

4. Measurable — How can I track my progress?

_____
_____
_____
_____

5. Sustainable — How will I sustain this over the long term?

_____
_____
_____
_____

★★★

1. Emotional — How do I want to feel?

_____
_____
_____
_____

2. Personal — Who do I want to be? How do I define the feeling of who I want to be?

_____
_____

_____
_____

3. Literal — What I am specifically going to do to feel and be that person?

_____
_____
_____
_____

4. Measurable — How can I track my progress?

_____
_____
_____
_____

5. Sustainable — How will I sustain this over the long term?

_____
_____
_____
_____

★★★

1. Emotional — How do I want to feel?

_____
_____
_____
_____

2. Personal — Who do I want to be? How do I define the feeling of who I want to be?

_____
_____
_____
_____

3. Literal — What I am specifically going to do to feel and be that person?

_____
_____
_____
_____

4. Measurable — How can I track my progress?

_____
_____

_____
_____

5.   Sustainable — How will I sustain this over the long term?

_____
_____
_____
_____

★★★

1.   Emotional — How do I want to feel?

_____
_____
_____
_____

2.   Personal — Who do I want to be? How do I define the feeling of who I want to be?

_____
_____
_____
_____

3. Literal — What I am specifically going to do to feel and be that person?

_____
_____
_____
_____

4. Measurable — How can I track my progress?

_____
_____
_____
_____

5. Sustainable — How will I sustain this over the long term?

_____
_____
_____
_____

★★★

Friction Points are the moments we're posed with an option, a time to make a choice. The more Friction Points between where you are and where you want to be to reach your goal, the less likely you are to get there.

The true secret to reaching any goal is to identify the Friction Points along the way and combat them ahead of time.

For each goal - list the potential Friction Points and how to combat them.

Goal:
Friction Point:
How I'll Combat:

Goal:

Friction Point:

How I'll Combat:

Goal:

Friction Point:

How I'll Combat:

Goal:
Friction Point:
How I'll Combat:

Goal:
Friction Point:
How I'll Combat:

Goal:
Friction Point:
How I'll Combat:

Goal:
Friction Point:
How I'll Combat:

Goal:
Friction Point:
How I'll Combat:

Goal:
Friction Point:
How I'll Combat:

Goal:

Friction Point:

How I'll Combat:

Goal:

Friction Point:

How I'll Combat:

So you want to be Successful? Great, same.

By now you've figured out how you want to feel and who you want to be.

You even have a plan to get there.

But where is there? How are you defining "success"?

Is it money in the bank? A new Birkin? A specific number of followers on Instagram?

There's no judgment here – it's your life and your definition of success.

How do I define success?

_____
_____
_____
_____
_____
_____
_____
_____
_____
_____
_____
_____
_____
_____

So, now you've clearly defined your success measure, what are you going to do about it?

Change jobs, pick up a side hustle, save spare change until you can buy that status symbol item, take a course on how to get more Instagram followers??

How are you going to track your progress?

Stop. This one is important.

Remember the momentum I told you about? This is where you find it. Whatever your goal is, you have got to make it trackable — figure out a way to see your progress over time using the habit trackers on the next few pages.

HABIT TRACKER

MONTH JAN FEB MAR APR MAY JUN JUL AUG SEP OCT NOV DEC

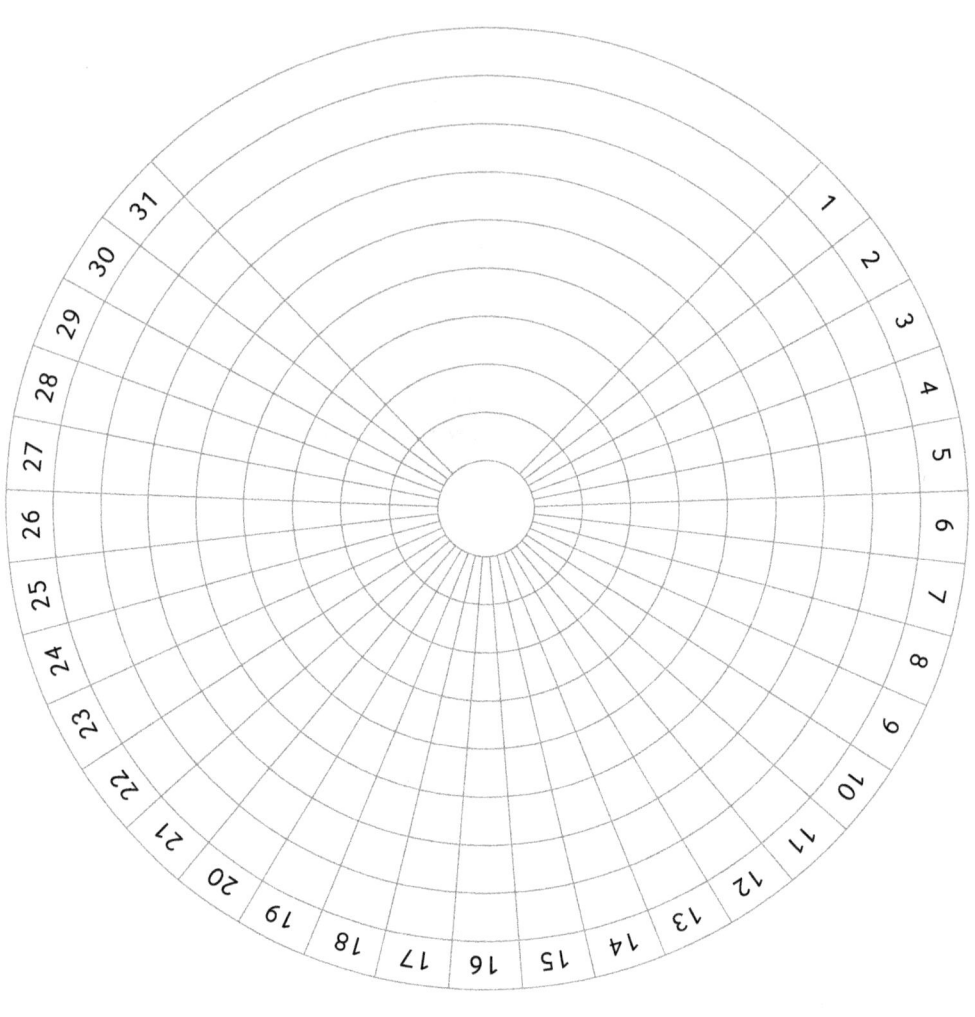

NOTES

HABIT TRACKER

MONTH   JAN   FEB   MAR   APR   MAY   JUN   JUL   AUG   SEP   OCT   NOV   DEC

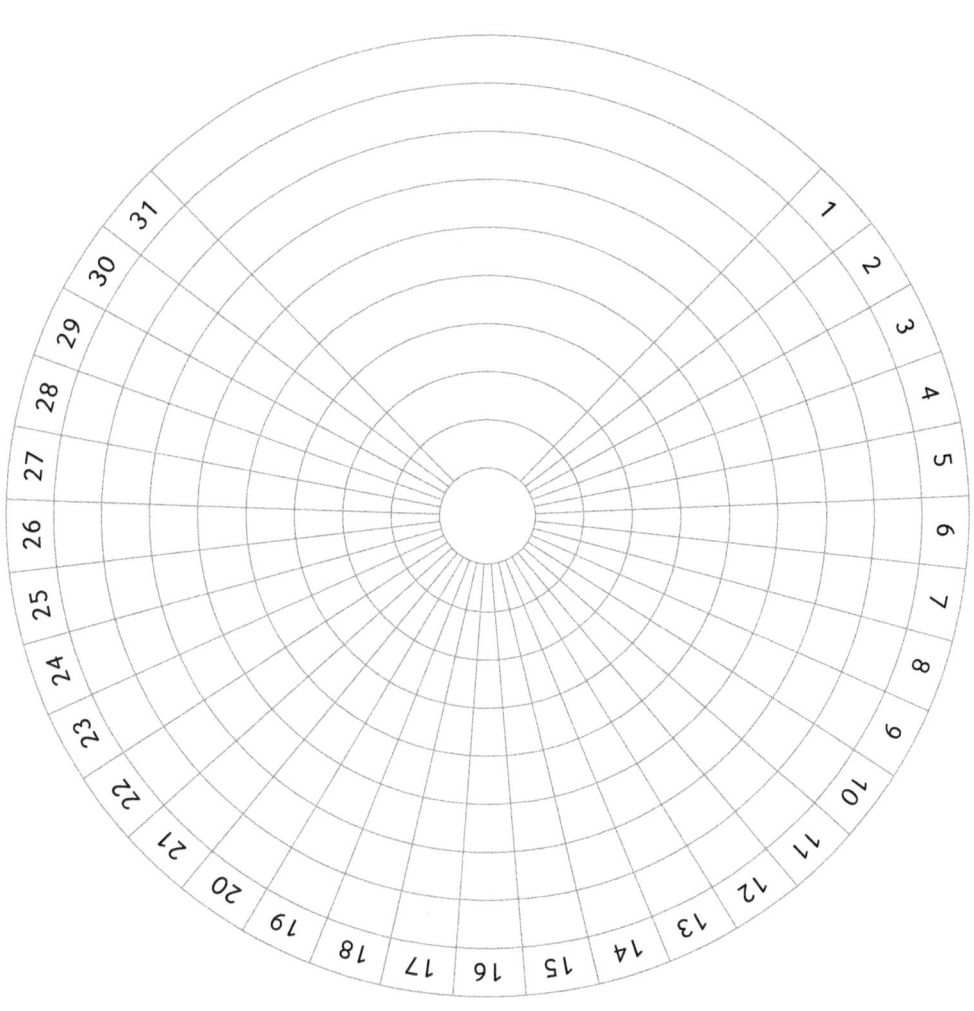

NOTES

HABIT TRACKER

MONTH JAN FEB MAR APR MAY JUN JUL AUG SEP OCT NOV DEC

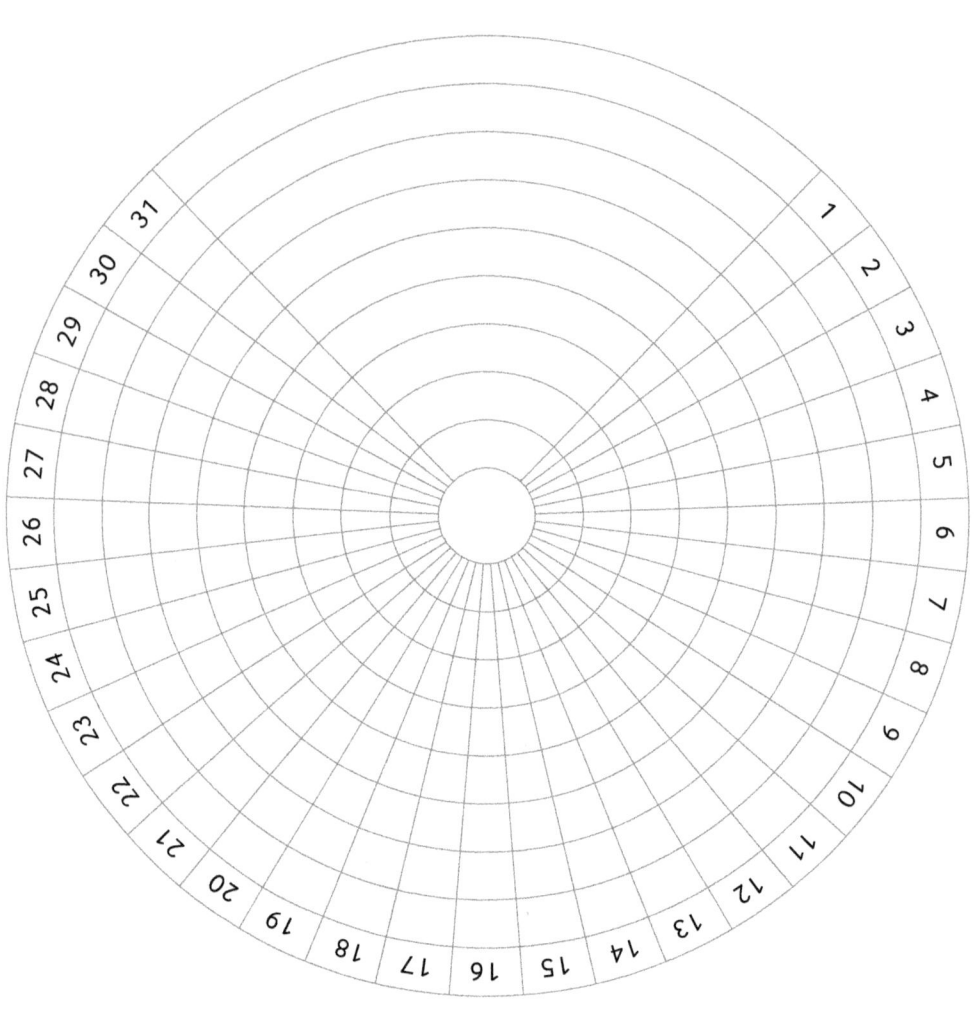

NOTES

HABIT TRACKER

MONTH   JAN   FEB   MAR   APR   MAY   JUN   JUL   AUG   SEP   OCT   NOV   DEC

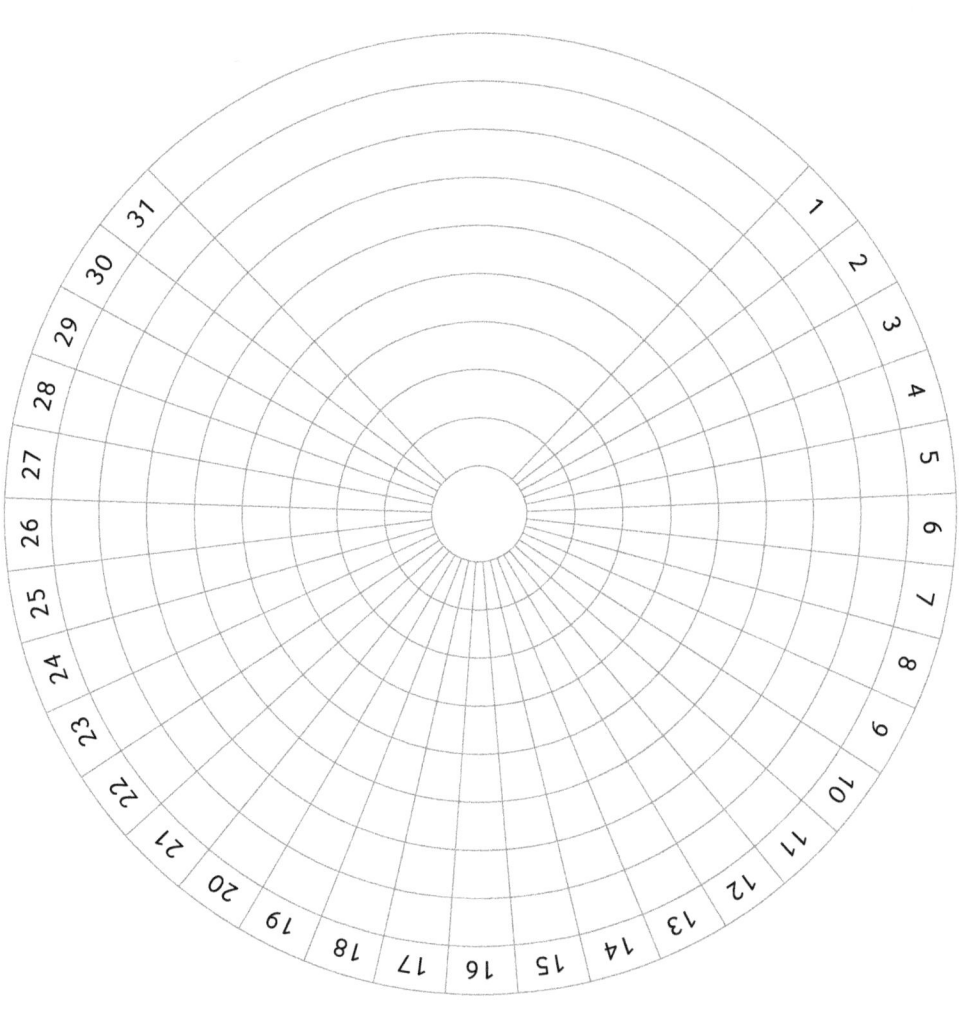

NOTES

HABIT TRACKER

MONTH JAN FEB MAR APR MAY JUN JUL AUG SEP OCT NOV DEC

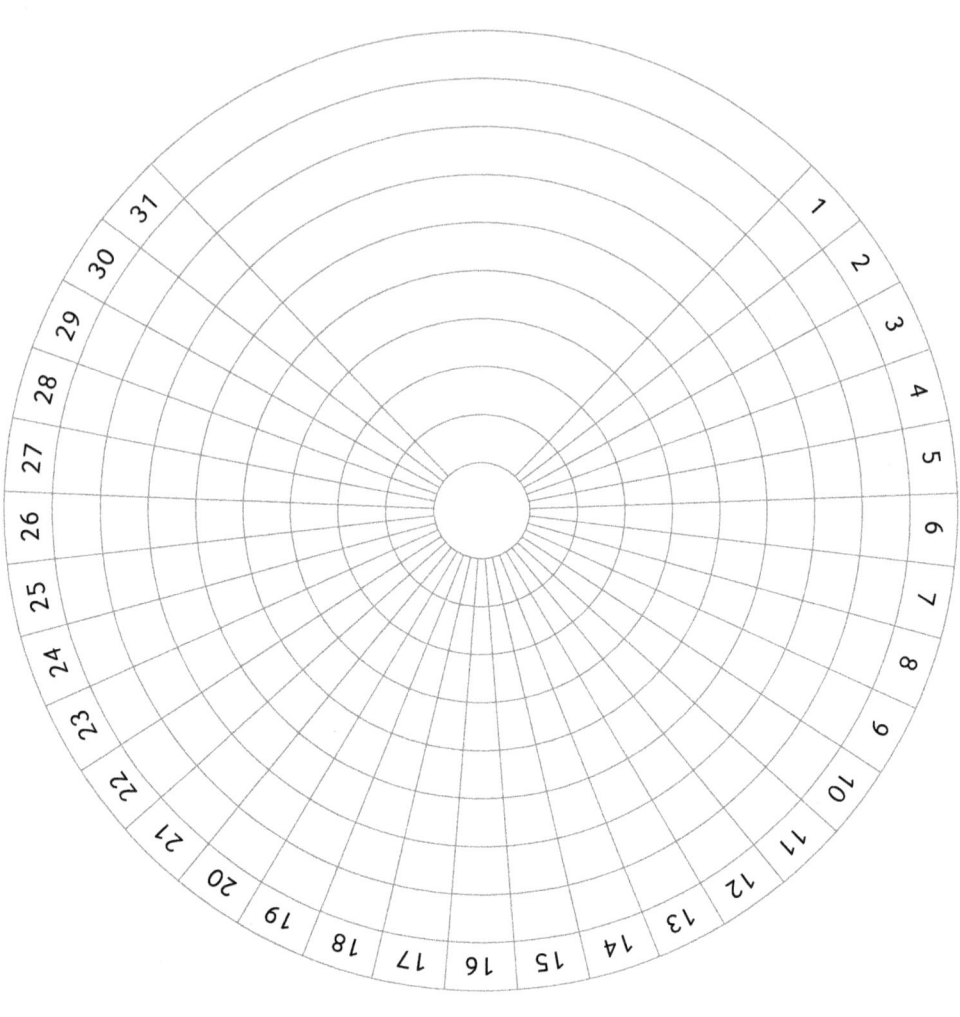

NOTES

HABIT TRACKER

MONTH   JAN   FEB   MAR   APR   MAY   JUN   JUL   AUG   SEP   OCT   NOV   DEC

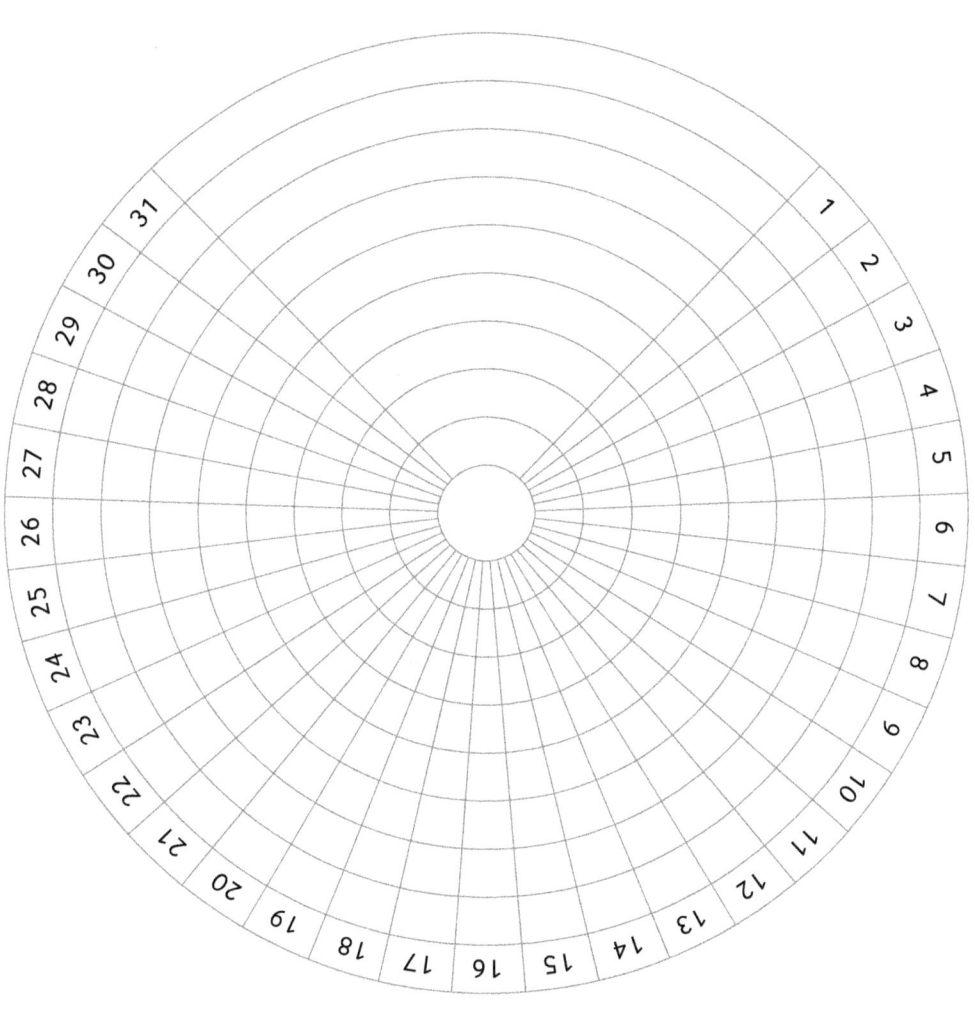

NOTES

www.ingramcontent.com/pod-product-compliance
Lightning Source LLC
Chambersburg PA
CBHW070108100426
42743CB00012B/2688